The Good Life

THE
GOOD

LIFE

Personal Expressions of Happiness by Paul McCartney, Helen Hayes, Boris Pasternak, Joan Kennedy, Richard Burton, Shirley Chisholm and many more

Selected by Shifra Stein

♔ Hallmark Editions

THE GOOD LIFE

Boris Pasternak:
SUCH A HAPPY LIFE

Life takes care of life. Man should devote his time and energy to his own activity. This was the philosophy of Russian writer Boris Pasternak, author of Doctor Zhivago. In this letter to his close friend Nina Tabidze, Pasternak considers his life—and the many happy times that made living good.

15 April 1951

...Nina, my best friend, my joy, I am ready for anything at any moment. But if I were no more, my life would be left behind, such a happy life, for which I am so grateful to heaven, a life which, like a book, was full of such quiet, concentrated meaning. What was the chief and fundamental thing about it? The example of my father's work, love of music..., two or three chords in my own writings, a night in the Russian countryside, the revolution, Georgia....

Albert Schweitzer:
LIFE'S BLESSINGS

Renowned humanitarian Albert Schweitzer found his life filled with many blessings, among them the affection of people the world over.

In my own life anxiety, trouble, and sorrow have been allotted to me at times in such abundant measure that had my nerves not been so strong, I must have broken down under the weight. Heavy is the burden of fatigue and responsibility which has lain upon me without a break for years. I have not much of my life for myself, not even the hours I should like to devote to my wife and child.

But I have had blessings too: that I am allowed to work in the service of mercy; that my work has been successful; that I receive from other people affection and kindness in abundance; that I have loyal helpers who identify themselves with my activity; that I enjoy a health which allows me to undertake most exhausting work; that I have a well-balanced temperament which varies little, and an energy which exerts itself with calmness and deliberation; and, finally, that I can recognize as such whatever happiness falls to my lot, accepting it also as a thing for which some thank offering is due from me.

Dustin Hoffman:
NEW YORK

Whether it be the Village, the East Side or the West Side, home to actor Dustin Hoffman is New York. It thrills him just to be there.

I think I have been preparing myself psychologically to live in New York all my life. I love New York; I consider it my home. Wherever I've lived in Manhattan, on the East Side or the West Side or in the Village, I've loved being able to walk to museums, theaters, restaurants. Every time I go out of the city and fly back and cab in from the airport, I get such a thrill out of being here. That's the only thing in my life I'd change if I could do it all over again; I'd have myself born in New York!

Joan Baez:
HOPE FOR MANKIND

*Despite our problems,
folk singer Joan Baez feels
there is good in mankind — good which
may one day be turned into hope
for the birth of true brotherhood.*

To state facts about the condition of mankind becomes hackneyed and boring, and we lose patience with hearing them. Not because they are not true, but because they are not real to us. They seem to be things out of our control. The truth is simply that we are living in the most violent, reckless, and deadly era the world has ever known. And we, the human race, have chosen to be as blind as snakes, as stubborn as asses, and dumber than cows.

And yet to look into the eyes of any man who is open and vulnerable for as much as one second, the world seems to turn suddenly into an unmapped ocean of innocence, hope, and beauty. A world in which man recognizes that he has a choice of how to live his life. He does not have to be a snake, ass, or cow, but a whole

8

person. If those moments can be nurtured, un-
derstood, and built upon rather than fearfully
labeled and swept away then there is truly hope
for mankind's survival and the birth of brotherhood.

The odds? Against.

The risks? High.

The reason to bother? The joy of living and
watching the flowering of love.

Pablo Casals:
THE TREE OF HUMANITY

*The truly important things in life—love,
beauty and one's own uniqueness—
are constantly being overlooked, laments cellist
Pablo Casals. He thinks the love of humanity
should extend past the borders of the mind
and encompass The Good Life for all.*

As a man, my first obligation is to the welfare
of my fellowmen. I will endeavor to meet this
obligation through music—the means which
God has given me—since it transcends lan-

guage, politics, and national boundaries. My contribution to world peace may be small. But at least I will have given all I can to an ideal I hold sacred.

Sometimes I look about me with a feeling of complete dismay. In the confusion that afflicts the world today, I see a disrespect for the very values of life. Beauty is all about us, but how many are blind to it!

Each second we live is a new and unique moment of the universe, a moment that never was before and will never be again. And what do we teach our children in school? We teach them that two and two make four and that Paris is the capital of France. When will we also teach them what they are? We should say to each of them: "Do you know what you are? You are a marvel. You are unique. In all of the world there is no other child exactly like you. In the millions of years that have passed, there has never been another child like you. And look at your body—what a wonder it is! Your legs, your arms, your cunning fingers, the way you move! You may become a Shakespeare, a Michelangelo, a Beethoven. You have the capacity for anything. Yes, you are a marvel. And when you grow up, can you then harm another who is,

like you, a marvel? You must cherish one another. You must work—we all must work—
to make this world worthy of its children."

The love of one's country is a natural thing.
But why should love stop at the border? We
are all leaves of a tree, and the tree is humanity.

Eleanor Roosevelt:
LEARNING AND LIVING

*One of the world's best loved
and most admired women, the late
Eleanor Roosevelt felt that learning and living
were synonymous in finding
The Good Life.*

Learning and living. But they are really the
same thing, aren't they? There is no experience
from which you can't learn something. When
you stop learning you stop living in any vital
and meaningful sense. And the purpose of life,
after all, is to live it, to taste experience to the
utmost, to reach out eagerly and without fear
for newer and richer experience.

You can do that only if you have curiosity, an unquenchable spirit of adventure. The experience can have meaning only if you understand it. You can understand it only if you have arrived at some knowledge of yourself, a knowledge based on a deliberately and usually painfully acquired self-discipline, which teaches you to cast out fear and frees you for the fullest experience of the adventure of life.

Many people seem to go through life without seeing. They do not know how to look around them. Only when you have learned that can you really continue to learn about people, about conditions, about your own locality.

If you can develop ability to see what you look at, to understand its meaning, to readjust your knowledge to this new information, you can continue to learn and to grow as long as you live and you'll have a wonderful time doing it.

Life is like a blanket too short. You pull it up and your toes rebel, you yank it down and shivers meander about your shoulder; but cheerful folks manage to draw their knees up and pass a very comfortable night. Marion Howard

Jonathan Miller, M.D.:
A MIRACULOUS CHRYSALIS

A downpour of rain, a hot, silent afternoon,

or a city blanketed in snow

serves to stimulate "the muscles of the mind,"

says physician-writer Jonathan Miller.

To him a mind-opening

awareness of the world is essential

if one is to enjoy life.

The world is a miraculous chrysalis which cracks open under the heat of attention, yielding angels which whir about your head like dragonflies....

You can sometimes get the effect in the middle of the English countryside, on a hot silent summer afternoon. Three o'clock seems about to go on forever, and the heat-stunned stillness seems like the edge of doomsday. All around, the trees stand ankle deep in the lifeblood of their own shadow, birdsong stops for a moment, the insect machinery switches off. The whole of creation sweats with expectation.

There is no knowing what the scene is about to deliver. In one sense it is irrelevant. The expectation is all; fulfillment can only be an anticlimax....

All I want is some device which keeps me constantly in touch with the bizarre "thereness" of the world in which I have been formed.

Fortunately, the world itself comes up with stimuli which jolt the mind in this direction. Once you are in practice, small changes of climate even will do the trick. There is nothing like a sudden wind, for example, to switch the mind into high gear. Or a sousing, catastrophic downpour of rain. Or a snowstorm when the whole city seems suddenly to have been seriously burned, then bandaged and consigned to a darkened invalid silence. The point is, once the muscles of the mind are in tune, very small changes of sensation, mood, climate, or interest can produce quite startling alterations in consciousness.

My life has taught me that if you are able to attain fully what it is that you want to achieve, that is the closest thing to happiness. Shelley Winters

Paul McCartney:
LIVE YOUR OWN LIFE

Ex-Beatle Paul McCartney finds his life filled with "ordinary things" that bring him great happiness. He enjoys them most when he does them spontaneously.

I love my life now because I'm doing much more ordinary things, and to me that brings great joy....

In New York, we go to Harlem on the subway—a great evening at the Apollo. We walk through Central Park after hours. You may find us murdered one day. Last time we went, it was snowy, like moonlight in Vermont—just fantastic. And I figure anyone who scares me, I scare him.

We try never to organize our lives very much. We do things on the spur of the moment.

I love to find that, even in this day of concrete, there are still alive horses and places where grass grows in unlimited quantities and sky has got clear air in it. Scotland has that. It's just there without anyone touching it. It just

grows. I'm relieved to find that it isn't all pollution. It isn't all the Hudson. It's not all the drug problem.

When we are in Scotland we plant stuff—vegetables—and we'll leave them there, and of their own volition they will push up. And not only will they push up and grow into something, but then they will be good to eat. To me that's an all-time thing. That's fantastic. How clever! Just that things push their own way up and they feed you.

So I think you've got to live your own life. That sounds like one of those statements, but it is, in fact, just very necessary to realize that. And particularly necessary for me. Or else someone else is going to be living part of your life for you.

We live only to discover beauty.
All else is a form of waiting. Kahlil Gibran

Life is something like this trumpet. If you don't put anything in it, you don't get anything out. And that's the truth. W. C. Handy

Joan Kennedy:
FRIENDSHIP

Though she has many of the material things thought of in relation to The Good Life, Joan Kennedy has discovered that friendship is what really makes life good.

Many people won't let those they love really know them, because they're afraid that if they show their true selves they won't be loved. I think it's good to know that you'll still be loved in spite of yourself, in spite of your faults....

Anything you care about you have to work at. I work at staying close to a few friends in Washington and Boston. These are friends to whom I can and do tell almost everything. Most of them are friends from my days at Manhattanville College. I think this has been my big discovery of the last few years — that I have a need for close relationships; I hadn't realized it before. It was usually fun-and-games relationships with me, I guess. People were pals, buddies, but not real friends. Now I know I want and need beautiful, continuing, intimate relationships.

Helen Hayes:
WALKING

Exploring a city or searching for solitude, walking is one of Helen Hayes' greatest joys.

I think you miss so much of a city when you just drive around. You must walk to get the feel, to be able to remember what you saw. It is only when I've walked around a place—stopped and studied and imagined—that I can close my eyes and return myself, at least in spirit, to where I was. Even in familiar places there are always new things to be seen.

When I want solitude, I go for a walk in the woods. When I go to see places, I like to encounter them as they were meant to be when they were built... throbbing with life, teeming with people, with noise and excitement.

One of my favorite walks, when I'm home in Nyack, is on the path along the Hudson River leading to Hook Mountain, that mysterious and wonderful-looking mountain with a bite out of its side where once were the quarries that supplied the brownstone for so many fashionable houses in New York. From my house on North Broadway it is about three miles up and back. And though I have done it for years —there were times when I did it every day—I have never tired of it. There seems always to be something new to watch on the river, something new to marvel at in the thickets and the woods.

M. F. K. Fisher:
THE WINE IS ALMOST PERFECT

Good wine, clean air, comfortable friends—for food writer M. F. K. Fisher, living is easy in the California sun.

I live in a good old wooden house, airy and alive at the end of its first century, in a small town somewhat older. Most of the people around me are wine makers from France and Italy, Switzerland and Germany. The soil in the California valley is volcanic ash, which settled down almost six million years ago when Mount Saint Helena blew off its top. The grapes it grows are eminently worth crushing, and the people who do it are right for my spirit. The air is always sweet, and the house smells pleasantly of food I like to cook and wine I like to pour. It is overfilled with pictures I want to look at often, and books I may want to reread, and furniture I like because it is used all the time, as it has been for many decades.

All this seems to have been of my choosing. There are many other ways to live, and even where I am, I could be dirty, or surly, or things I am uncomfortable in contemplating. I do not say that if I could, or had to, start a new life, I would choose this way. But this is the way my past, my education, my environment all taught me to live now. I could never say that I like all of my pattern, and I recognize that I am perhaps too cozily removed from the rapacious activities of other parts of my planet Earth. But I am here. The wine is almost perfect....

There are two things to aim at in life; first, to get what you want; and, after that, to enjoy it. Only the wisest of mankind achieve the second.
                                          Logan Pearsall Smith

Lady Bird Johnson:
THE HAPPY TIMES

For the wife of the ex-president,
The Good Life might be anything
from entertaining at a Texas barbecue
to attending elegant Washington
parties. But for Lady Bird Johnson,
the simple pleasures are the best.

I like being real tired from getting the last weed out of the zinnia bed, and finally sitting down with a glass of lemonade to see how pretty the flowers look. I like sitting on the back of the boat at twilight, down home on the Llano River, watching the sun go down behind Pack Saddle Mountain. If that won't bring joy to your soul, you're past saving.

Then there's the joy of getting your desk clean and knowing that all your letters are answered, and you can see the wood on it again. There's something real satisfying about working and having gotten it done. And there's something equally satisfying about just sitting around the kitchen table and having a glass of milk with Lynda Bird, while she tells me all her problems, and I feel that we've gotten to that intimate little moment of true meeting. Those are the times when I am really happy.

Helen and Scott Nearing:
SIEMPRE MEJOR

*Many dream of leaving the city
to begin a life of homesteading
in the country. Helen and Scott Nearing
are two people who actually did it,
giving up everything to start a new life.
With their pioneer spirit, they made
the country life bloom for them.*

Living is a business in which we all engage. In the course of the day, there are certain things we must do—for example, breathe. There are also things we may do or may decide not to do —such as stay home and bake a cake, or go out and visit a friend. The center of life routine is surrounded by a circumference of choice. There is the vocation which provides livelihood, and the avocations which thrive on leisure and surplus energy.

We may state the issue in another way—whatever the nature of one's beliefs, one's personal conduct may either follow the belief pattern or diverge from it. Insofar as it diverges, it helps produce unwanted results. At the same time, it splits practice away from theory and divides the personality against itself. The most harmonious life is one in which theory and practice are unified.

From this it follows that each moment, hour, day, week and year should be treated as an occasion—another opportunity to live as well as possible, in accordance with the old saying "Tomorrow is a new day" or the new Mexican greeting "Siempre mejor" (always better) in place of the conventional "Buenos dias" (good day). With body in health, emotions in balance, mind in tune and vision fixed on a better life and a better world, life, individually and collectively, is already better.

On this point we differ emphatically with many of our friends and acquaintances who say, in effect, "Never mind how we live today; we are in this dog-eat-dog social system and we may as well get what we can out of it. But tomorrow, in a wiser, more social and more humane world, we will live more rationally, more economically, more efficiently, more socially." Such talk is nonsense. As we live in the present, so is our future shaped, channeled and largely determined.

Viewed in a long perspective, our Vermont project was a personal stopgap, an emergency expedient. But in the short view it was a way of preserving self-respect and of demonstrating to the few who were willing to observe, listen and participate, that life in a dying acquisitive culture can be individually and socially purposeful, creative, constructive and deeply rewarding....

I repeatedly discover and savor life in my daily search for personal wholeness, personal integrity. In that sense, life itself is the good life.
Jacqueline Grennan Wexler

Charles de Gaulle:
A SOURCE OF NEW ARDOR

The late General de Gaulle, president of France, discovered The Good Life far from the whirl of government and power and politics. Instead, he found his "secret solace" in the secluded acres surrounding his home.

In the tumult of men and events, solitude was my temptation; now it is my friend. What other satisfaction can be sought once you have confronted history?

Silence fills my house. From the corner room where I spend most of my daylight hours, I look out far into the west. There is nothing to obstruct my view for some fifteen kilometers. Above the plain and the woods, my eyes follow the long slopes descending toward the valley of the Aube, then the heights of the slope opposite. From a rise in the garden, I look down

on the wild depths where the forest envelops the tilled land like the sea beating on a promontory. I watch the night cover the landscape. Then, looking up at the stars, I steep myself in the insignificance of earthly things.

On our little property—I have walked around it fifteen thousand times—the trees, stripped by the cold, rarely fail to turn green again, and the flowers my wife has planted bloom once more each spring. The village houses are decrepit, but suddenly laughing girls and boys come out of their doors. When I walk to one of the nearby woods...their solemn depths fill me with nostalgia; but suddenly the song of a bird, the sun through the leaves, or the buds of a thicket remind me that ever since it has existed on earth, life wages a battle it has never lost. Then I feel a secret solace passing through me. Since everything eternally begins anew, what I have done will sooner or later be a source, a new ardor after I have gone.

A person does not find *life worth living; he* makes *life worth living.*   Rev. Howard J. Brown

Storm Jameson:
DEJA VU

*A nostalgic look at her childhood
fills novelist Storm Jameson
with happiness as she recalls
the day she spent making a calendar
to please her mother.
Sometimes the past seems like
the best life of all.*

I am writing this at a table of plain wood. Just now, when I ran my hand along the edge, a tiny splinter caught the edge of my palm. Pulling it out, I felt a wave of happiness, even gaiety. It had not come from one of those exultant moments when, dropping with sleep, alone in some cold room, I stumbled on words that I believed came from a center of my body rather than my brain, but it belonged to that family. Another instant and I had it...I am in the kitchen of my mother's house, facing an iron range, the curtains drawn across the window on my right, one weak lamp throwing its yellow hoop on the square of cardboard under my hand. The calendar I am making for my mother in the hope of pleasing her and being praised has the months, days, figures copied in red and green ink, and the wide margins filled in with an intricate pattern of small blue flowers, each petal painted separately with the point of the finest brush, scores of flowers, hundreds of petals. Slowly adding flower to flower, stopping only for a second to pull out the splinter my left hand has picked up from the rough edge of the table, I am happy, my God how happy.

Surely, somewhere, it is still alive, the gaiety, the simple patience?

Of course. How else could you live?

Peg Bracken:
MIDDLE AGE

Somewhere between the age of forty-five and sixty-five, author and magazine writer Peg Bracken is having the time of her life.

I would like to report...on Middle Age, which I find interesting and likable country. But I want to make it clear that this is a personal report, and undoubtedly prejudiced.

By Middle Age I mean...the years from forty-five to sixty-five, give or take a few on either end. This isn't quite twilight, and certainly not bedtime, but, more aptly, the cocktail hour, or, depending on one's persuasion, high tea.

Middle Age is when your chickens come home to roost, all right—all your past sins and indiscretions. But surely there were some good little chickens, too; surely one committed some discretions right along with the indiscretions. Surely the orange juice registers, right along with the gin.

A great thing about Middle Age is that one is usually in charge of his own life more completely than ever before. This includes both little and big things, both equally satisfying.

With Middle Age, you can start being honest about what you don't want to do and undoubtedly won't do.

I know, now, that I'll never read *Remembrance of Things Past*, and I know I'll never have the patience to pound the whole half-cupful of flour into the Swiss steak, and I don't really care.

I know I'll never understand the capital-gains tax, and I don't care about that either.

I'm pretty sure I'll never get proposed to in a gondola (as well as a lot of other places), but that's all right with me. I know I'll never fly a helicopter or speak French like a native of anywhere but Missouri. Or ever achieve that splendid, perfectly-put-together look, because I'll always have a handbag or something else in some evasive color I got because it would go with everything and as a result doesn't go with anything.

As for memorizing "Ode to a Nightingale" or lists of battle dates, I know I could if I had to pass a test on it tomorrow. However, a truly glorious thing about Middle Age is knowing that I don't. The sort of tests you get at this point aren't the kind you have to study for, and that's fine with me. It's a lovely thing to know you can choose your own books or none, or your own alley, job, path, playground...just so you pick one to stay alive with, because there are probably so many good years ahead.

Althea Gibson:
TO BE SOMEBODY

*Tennis champion Althea Gibson
has what she wants out of life —
her identity and the respect of her
friends and fans.*

My pleasures and interests are simple. I have no lofty, overpowering ambition. All I want is to be able to play tennis, sing, sleep peacefully, have three square meals a day, a regular income, and no worries. I don't feel any need to be a King Midas with a whole string of people hanging on me to be supported. I don't want to be put on a pedestal. I just want to be reasonably successful and live a normal life with all the conveniences to make it so. I think I've already got the main thing I've always wanted, which is to be somebody, to have identity.

Life consists not in holding good cards but in playing those you do hold well.   Josh Billings

Senator Robert F. Kennedy:
TINY RIPPLES OF HOPE

The late Senator Robert F. Kennedy believed that by helping others we help ourselves. It was important to him that everyone take part in building a Good Life for all men.

Few will have the greatness to bend history itself, but each of us can work to change a small portion of events, and in the total of all those acts will be written the history of this generation. Thousands of Peace Corps volunteers are making a difference in isolated villages and city slums in dozens of countries. Thousands of unknown men and women in Europe resisted the occupation of the Nazis and many died, but all added to the ultimate strength and freedom of their countries. It is from numberless diverse acts of courage and belief that human history is shaped. Each time a man stands up for an ideal, or acts to improve the lot of others, or strikes out against injustice, he sends forth a tiny ripple of hope, and crossing each other from a million different centers of energy and daring, those ripples build a current that can sweep down the mightiest walls of oppression and resistance.

Corita Kent:
DIG FOR THE RICHNESS

The intricate silkscreenings of the ex-nun

once known as Sister Corita

have become famous all over the world.

For her The Good Life is simply

being good.

Maybe there is no "good life"
but only trying to be good
(and trying not to kill)
trying to walk the tightrope
to keep the balance
to hold the tension
of dark and light
joy and pain—
learning enough to be a fool

38

a clown
to carry the pain and
help others to laugh so that
they can bear their pain.

And at some time
in your life
trying to be good
may be to stop running
and take time
(no use waiting to find it
or to kill it)
to be quiet
and discover who you are
and where you've been
uncovering layer by layer
all your dark levels —
to look at the black in yourself
and dig for the richness in it —
mysterious light that comes
out of darkness —
trying to recognize
your own darkness
to face it
and work it into the light
instead of putting it
into others
and killing them.

Richard Burton:
GREAT FUN

*The Good Life
for actor Richard Burton?
Travel, fine books and being
married to his beautiful wife
Elizabeth. He says it
couldn't be better.*

At our house in Switzerland we don't have any help at all. Elizabeth does the cooking and I do all the cleaning. I rather enjoy it. It's the touch of the feminine in my nature. I suppose I like washing dishes and stuff like that. All those scourers and detergents. But I must be left alone.

We don't bother about clothes. Elizabeth slops about in jeans until she suddenly decides to dress up. Then even if we stay in she'll put on something exotic—sometimes erotic! Generally speaking, if we are alone, we don't eat out much. We have great fun in our house at Puerto Vallarta, Mexico. Whenever a boat arrives from the States, about two thousand people pour out onto the quay, pile into the waiting lines of

taxis and mini-buses and drive straight to our house. They stand outside and take photographs.

Ideally we'd like to spend six months in Mexico and six months in Europe. We've discovered just how much we love Puerto Vallarta, having been there on and off for nearly seven years. But sometimes the lust for Europe is too great. We start dreaming about roast pork and crackling, and we long to get back.

The whole family is mad about horses. About five months ago a very rich Mexican gave Elizabeth a magnificent white stallion, and she spent a lot of time riding. She might breed horses, for all I know. As long as she leaves me in my book-lined room, I don't mind.

Don't refuse to go on an occasional wild goose chase; that is what wild geese are made for.
Henry S. Haskins

Yael Dayan:
LIFE ITSELF

At 19, the daughter of Israel's military hero fought in her father's army. Now in her thirties, Yael Dayan wants the world to forget war and start enjoying life.

The Good Life, in capitals, has a quality for me now, its distance realized only when I hear a news broadcast or read a newspaper.

It then becomes the absence rather than the presence of things: Not to see names of 18-year-old boys framed in black....Not to lose sons, husbands, fathers in a war which is endless and yet inevitable....Not to breathe the tense, heavy air of an isolated country fighting for survival....Not to look at my son and wonder whether he, too, will have to fight for what elsewhere is taken for granted—the right to live on his land....

This is my microcosmos. This is why for us the Good Life is simply *life itself.*

Coretta Scott King:
MY BROTHER'S SISTER
AND MY SISTER'S SISTER

Devoted to peace and justice,

the wife of the late

Martin Luther King, Jr.

sees The Good Life as a world filled

with compassion and concern for

our fellowman.

Too long have we been our brother's keeper; in the '70s, I would hope to become my brother's sister and my sister's sister. I would like to see a slowing down and perhaps a reversal of the present trends toward polarization—black and white, young and old, the rich becoming richer and the poor getting poorer. May we learn from the convulsions of the '60s the lessons needed for the '70s: that our youth are trying to show us our hypocrisy; that black people must know who they are before they can become equal participants in a society now dominated by whites; that violence and the mood it creates can destroy all of us; that the

45

underprivileged, or differently privileged, want to share in the American Dream; and that our nation can endure during the last third of this century only as one nation.

I pray that the kinds of power we discovered in the '60s—the power of youth, the power of the ballot, the power of group solidarity, the power of unselfish giving—can be translated in the '70s into the good life for many, many more of us, a world full of compassion and concern.

Phyllis McGinley:
A GOOD DAY

Living life one day at a time and being aware of each day's pleasures—that is the secret of happiness to this prize winning poet.

A good day is the most I dare define. Let it contain no unkindnesses, only a few homespun pleasures, and so far as a housewife like me is concerned, the soul can clap its hands and sing.

A good day is waking after eight solid hours

of sleep to find the sun shining through windows that have lately been washed and curtains freshly laundered; and to know on the instant of rising exactly what to get from the market for dinner.

It is keeping an appointment with the dentist to learn, at the end of the ordeal, that one's gums are solid as cement and there isn't a cavity in sight.

It is picking up the mail at the back door to discover that instead of bills and throwaways addressed to Occupant, the postman has delivered a letter from a friend.

The papers may be full of wars and rumors of wars and disasters on land and sea. But they depress me only momentarily if household news is cheerful. I can go whistling down the stairs because of a compliment from my husband or a reaffirmation that my daughters are happy in their jobs and marriages. I can live brightly for a week on recollections of the Saturday party we attended where everyone was not only a friend but agreed with me about politics, books, morality, and the necessity of applying superphosphate to the soil around rose beds. The good life consists of such rejoicings.

Walter Matthau:
HOW TO HAVE A HAPPY LIFE

It's a rocky road to riches and happiness, especially if you're a compulsive gambler who once lost $183,000 in two weeks betting on spring-training baseball games. Walter Matthau curbs his gambling now, and has found a Good Life that includes wealth, stardom and happiness.

It's a sure thing, he says, if you follow this basic guideline.

(1) Never bet on spring-training baseball games.
(2) Never play pinochle in partnership with anyone named Schultz.
(3) Take acting lessons at the New School.
(4) Divorce your first wife.
(5) Give up smoking.
(6) Always accept any role offered to you in any Broadway production of any Neil Simon play.
(7) Always agree to take a percentage of the

profits instead of a salary when asked to act in a movie, especially any film version of any Neil Simon play.

(8) Be happy, even though brought up in abject poverty, abandoned by your father and plagued by a strong dislike of Barbra Streisand.

Follow these eight principles and you surely can't miss.

Joyce Carol Oates:
THE ACT OF LOVING

This vibrant young novelist
finds a galaxy of Good Lives
here on earth—each one filled
to the brim with love.

in love
we are drawn in a long curve
like the rising of light
across the photographed globe

in love
we taste other mouths
indifferent

original
in every earthly touch
in love we repeat motions
we repeat love
we repeat our rising of love
like the fierce scanning of light
across the moving earth

There is no good "life" here on earth, but many good lives—the possibility of a galaxy of good lives, each holy....The good life for me is equal to love, to loving. What is there to say about the miraculous verb "to love" after so many centuries of loving?

Writing of love, ideally, as I do in the poem that has been inspired by this essay, I am thinking of any object outside ourselves that is worthy of our deepest commitment....I am thinking of the many ways of love: of creativity in all its forms, which is a generous and sometimes devastating love, whether it consists of the writing of poetry or novels or the production of works of visual art or the slow, careful cultivation of a family, the creation of anything that lifts us from ourselves, forcing us out of ourselves.

The good life exists, here on earth: it exists in the act of loving.

Shirley Chisholm:
THE PROMISE

Congresswoman Shirley Chisholm says that America's hope for the future lies in its potential for good. If that potential is realized, perhaps we all will enjoy The Good Life.

I don't measure America by its achievement, but by its potential. There are still many things that we haven't tried—that I haven't tried—to change the way our present system operates. I haven't exhausted the opportunities for action in the course I'm pursuing. If I ever do, I cannot at this point imagine what to do next.

We need men and women who have far greater abilities and far broader appeal than I will ever have, but who have my kind of independence —who will dare to declare that they are free of the old ways that have led us wrong, and who owe nothing to the traditional concentrations of capital and power that have subverted this nation's ideals....

There must be a new coalition of all Americans—black, white, red, yellow and brown, rich and poor—who are no longer willing to allow their rights as human beings to be infringed upon by anyone else, for any reason. We must join together to insist that this nation deliver on the promise it made, nearly 200 years ago, that every man be allowed to be a man. I feel an incredible urgency that we must do it now.

Dag Hammarskjöld:
A BRIDGE FOR OTHERS

What is the true purpose of man?

The late secretary—general to the

United Nations believed man was created

to be a free, responsible individual

whose goal in life it was to help others.

Hunger is my native place in the land of the passions. Hunger for fellowship, hunger for righteousness—for a fellowship founded on righteousness, and a righteousness attained in fellowship.

Only life can satisfy the demands of life. And this hunger of mine can be satisfied for the simple reason that the nature of life is such that I can realize my individuality by becoming a bridge for others, a stone in the temple of righteousness.

Don't be afraid of yourself, live your individuality to the full—but for the good of others. Don't copy others in order to buy fellowship, or make convention your law instead of living the righteousness.

To become free and responsible. For this alone was man created, and he who fails to take the Way which could have been his shall be lost eternally.

Do not look back. And do not dream about the future, either. It will neither give you back the past, nor satisfy your other daydreams. Your duty, your reward—your destiny—are *here* and *now*.

What I really want is to be pregnant and unemployed.
                                        Goldie Hawn

Jessamyn West:
FOUR CORNERSTONES

The well-known author
of The Friendly Persuasion finds great
joy in her family, her privacy,
the world of nature
and her work.

My good life has four cornerstones: family, words on paper (this means books and writing), the world of nature (weeds, wind, buzzards, clouds), and privacy.

Perhaps everyone's good life would include family, or what constitutes family for them. For a woman the best as contrasted with the merely good life exists when she loves a person or persons and can make them happy by her being and doing.

My good life of books and pen, privacy and the country might be the last kind of life most people would call good. Yet everyone, I think, would want what they bring me: Joy. Excitement. Contentment. Yes, even ecstasy. Maybe what I have been describing is the "great" life.

And maybe the good life can exist only when it occasionally opens out into areas of greatness: areas of great joy, great satisfaction. For everyone, that is.

The four cornerstones might be a little flat without a spire. Let this, then, be the spire. (Strange Quaker meetinghouse though it will look.) I do not wish upon you my good life. I wish for you what my good life brings to me.

A good life is like a good play—it has to have a satisfying and exciting third act.

Ethel Barrymore

For most men life is a search for the proper manila envelope in which to get themselves filed.

Clifton Fadiman

Artur Rubinstein:
ENJOY LIFE

Famed pianist Artur Rubinstein finds fulfillment in sharing his talent with others. To him the essence of life is doing something truly important to benefit humanity.

I live by one principle: Enjoy life with no conditions! People say, "If I had your health, if I had your money, oh, I would enjoy myself." It is not true. I would be happy if I were lying sick in a hospital bed. It must come from the inside. That is the one thing I hope I have contributed to my children, by example and by talk: to make no conditions, to understand that life is a wonderful thing and to enjoy it, every day, to the full.

To me the world is divided into two kinds of people: those who are conscious and those who are unconscious. To me there is no difference among men when it comes to their color,

their race, their religion; they are all equal. Only the degree of their awareness of the world they live in, of the joy and the pleasure of living, of the need of sharing that awareness with others and bringing it to their fellowmen (if they happen to be fortunate enough to have talent) is a measure of this difference.

During my long life I have learned one lesson: that the most important thing is to realize *why* one is alive—and I think it is not only to build bridges or tall buildings or make money, but to do something truly important, to do something for humanity. To bring joy, hope, to make life richer for the spirit because you have been alive, that is the most important thing.

Lin Yutang:
TRULY HAPPY MOMENTS

Author of My Country and My People, Lin Yutang offers what he has learned about the happiness of daily living.

To me,...the truly happy moments are: when I get up in the morning after a night of perfect sleep and sniff the morning air and there is an expansiveness in the lungs, when I feel inclined to inhale deeply and there is a fine sensation of movement around the skin and muscles of the chest, and when therefore, I am fit for work; or when I hold a pipe in my hand and rest my legs on a chair, and the tobacco burns slowly and evenly; or when I am traveling on a summer day, my throat parched with thirst, and I see a beautiful clear spring, whose very sound makes me happy, and I take off my socks and shoes and dip my feet in the delightful, cool water; or when after a perfect dinner I lounge in an armchair, when there is no one I hate to look at in the company and conversation rambles off at a light pace to an unknown destination, and I am spiritually and physically at peace with the world; or when on a summer afternoon I see black clouds gathering on the horizon and know for certain a July shower is coming in a quarter of an hour, but being ashamed to be seen going out into the rain without an umbrella, I hastily set out to meet the shower halfway across the fields and come home drenched through and through and tell my family that I was simply caught by the rain.

Marya Mannes:
SAVORING WHAT IS

Outspoken social critic,

author and television commentator

Marya Mannes believes that

our small pleasures add up

to a most rewarding life.

The good life exists only when you stop wanting a better one. It is the condition of savoring what is, rather than longing for what might be. ...The itch for things—so brilliantly injected by those who make them and sell them—is in effect a virus draining the soul of contentment. A man never earns enough, a woman is never beautiful enough, clothes are never new enough, the house is never furnished enough, the food is never fancy enough.

There is a point at which salvation lies in stepping off the escalator, of saying, Enough: What I have will do, what I make of it is up to me.

When you ask of this self More and Better, of what earthly importance is a new slipcover?

Or, say, the place where you live is dark much of the day because it is on a low floor in a city. Black dirt sifts through the windows, and they often shake with the blast of horns. But twice a day the sun wheels through them, makes abstract patterns on the walls, irradiates a bowl, warms old wood, and excites the heart. The good life is the ability to relish the small pleasures even if you are denied the great ones.

Set in Crown Roman and Jeanette script,
both designed exclusively for Hallmark Editions
by Hermann Zapf.
Printed on Hallmark Buff Vellux paper.
Designed by Lilian Weytjens.